I0815532

★★★★★

MLB TEAMS

Seattle MARINERS

KENNY ABDO

Fly!
An Imprint of Abdo Zoom
abdobooks.com

abdobooks.com

Published by Abdo Zoom, a division of ABDO, P.O. Box 398166, Minneapolis, Minnesota 55439.

Printed in the United States of America, North Mankato, Minnesota.
102025
012026

Photo Credits: AP Images, Getty Images, Shutterstock
Production Contributors: Kenny Abdo, Jennie Forsberg, Grace Hansen
Design Contributors: Candice Keimig, Neil Klinepier

Library of Congress Control Number: 2025936807

Publisher's Cataloging-in-Publication Data

Names: Abdo, Kenny, author.
Title: Seattle Mariners / by Kenny Abdo
Description: Minneapolis, Minnesota : Abdo Zoom, 2026 | Series: MLB teams | Includes online resources and index.
Identifiers: ISBN 9798384940326 (lib. bdg.) | ISBN 9798384941088 (ebook) | ISBN 9798384941460 (read-to-me ebook)
Subjects: LCSH: Seattle Mariners (Baseball team)--Juvenile literature. | Baseball teams--Juvenile literature. | Professional sports--Juvenile literature. | Sports franchises--Juvenile literature. | Major League Baseball (Organization)--Juvenile literature.
Classification: DDC 796.357--dc23

Table of CONTENTS

MARINERS

With power and grit, the Seattle Mariners sail into every game ready to win!

MARINERS
44

With star players, **record**-breaking moments, and a deep love for the game, the Mariners have made waves that unite fans all across Washington!

BATTER UP!

The Seattle Mariners joined the **American League (AL)** in 1977. The team got its first win just three games into the season. But that was one of few highlights for the 1977 Mariners. Seattle fans were thrilled to have a Major League Baseball (MLB) team, but building a winner was going to take some time.

Seatt
1

In the 1980s, the Mariners put together some talented teams. Alvin Davis won **Rookie** of the Year in 1984 after hitting 27 home runs. By the end of the decade, Ken Griffey Jr. joined the team and proved his skill by smashing a home run in his first at-bat!

11

In 1995, the Mariners adopted the motto "Refuse to Lose." The team's strong performance at the end of the season got them to the playoffs. They faced the Yankees in the **AL Division** Series. Game 5 was the biggest in Mariners history. Edgar Martinez hit a game-winning **double** to move on!

GRAND SLAMS

The Mariners won 116 games during the 2001 season, tying the Cubs' record for most wins in a year. Ichiro Suzuki won MVP and **Rookie** of the Year! The team reached the **AL** Championship Series but lost to the Yankees in five games.

MARINERS

SEATTLE

The Mariners missed the playoffs for many years after 2001. But young stars brought fresh energy to the team. Félix Hernández took the mound in 2005 and became one of the best pitchers in baseball. By 2010, he led the league in **ERA** and won the **Cy Young Award**!

SEATTLE
17

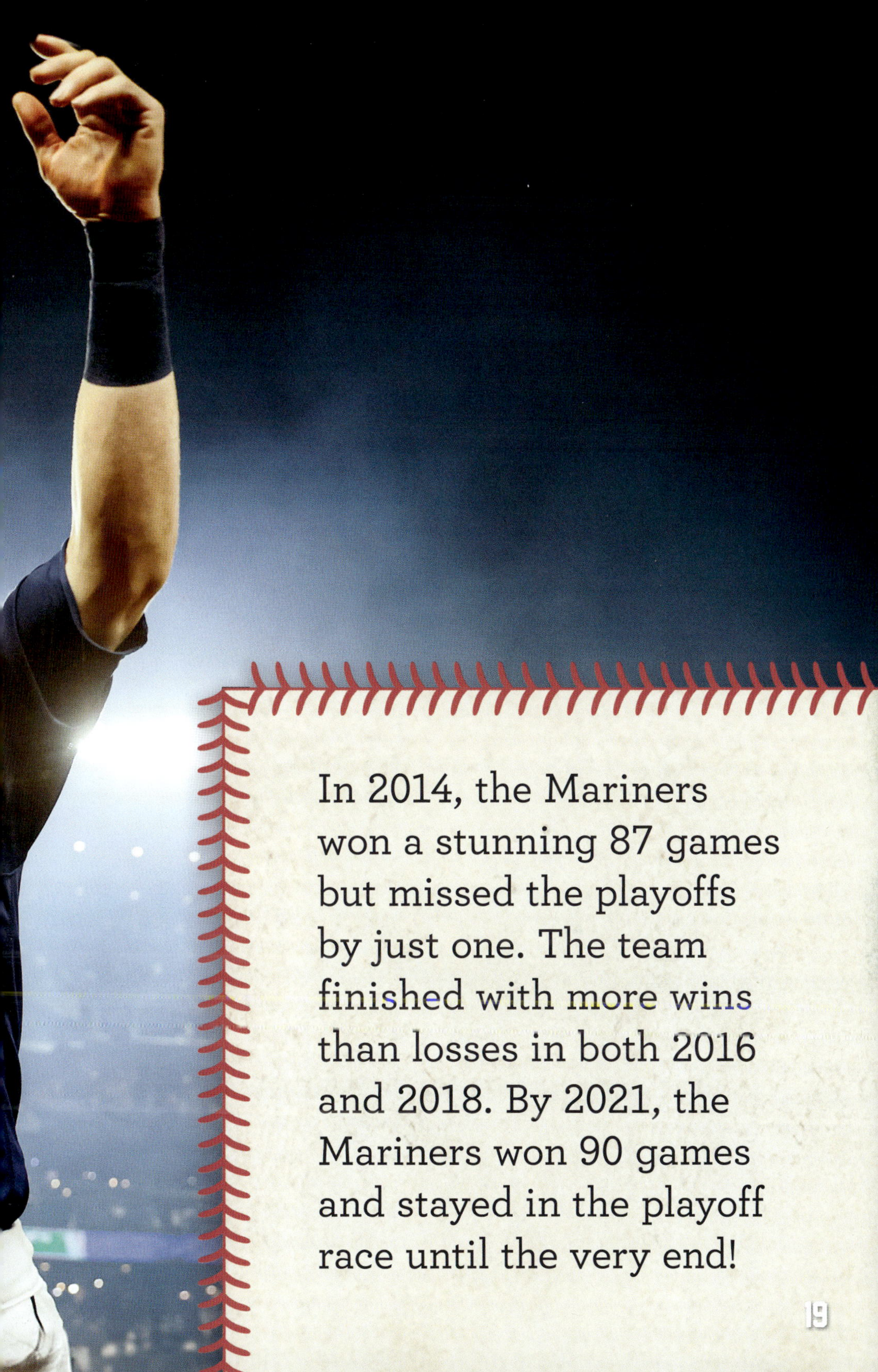

In 2014, the Mariners won a stunning 87 games but missed the playoffs by just one. The team finished with more wins than losses in both 2016 and 2018. By 2021, the Mariners won 90 games and stayed in the playoff race until the very end!

In 2022, the Mariners made the playoffs for the first time in over 20 years. The team beat the Blue Jays and moved on to the **Division** Series. That season, Julio Rodríguez made his **debut** and brought major talent to the roster. By 2025, Rodríguez had hit more than 110 home runs and stolen more than 112 bases for the Mariners.

MARINERS

The Mariners overcame a rough start to achieve great success in the 2025 season. J.P. Crawford found his sweet spot in hitting and **plate discipline**. Catcher Cal Raleigh had a **record**-setting 60-home run season.

The Mariners went on to win their first **AL** West title since 2001. They advanced to the AL Championship Series, but had a heartbreaking finish in Game 7 against Toronto. Still, Seattle was proud of its team.

HALL OF FAME

Ken Griffey Jr. was a superstar for the 1990s Mariners. He hit 417 home runs with Seattle and made ten **All-Star** teams. Griffey's smooth swing and catches made him one of the game's brightest stars. He was named to the Baseball Hall of Fame in 2016.

GRIFFEY
24

MARINERS

Edgar Martinez spent his entire career with the Mariners. He finished with a .312 batting average and won two batting titles. Martinez's famous **double** in 1995 helped Seattle win its first playoff series. He was named to the Baseball Hall of Fame in 2019.

Nobody had a bigger impact on the 2001 Mariners than **rookie** Ichiro Suzuki. He had speed around the bases, a controlled swing, and an accurate throwing arm. And he never seemed to slow down after that. Suzuki went on a 20-game hitting streak seven different times throughout his career. He joined the Baseball Hall of Fame in 2025.

GLOSSARY

All Star – a team consisting of athletes chosen as the best at their positions from all teams in a league or region.

American League (AL) – one of two 15-team leagues that make up MLB.

Cy Young Award – an annual American baseball award given to the best pitcher in each of the two MLB leagues.

debut – a first appearance in public.

division – a number of teams grouped together in a sport for competitive purposes.

double – a type of hit where the batter safely reaches second base on a single play.

Earned-Run Average (ERA) – the average number of earned runs per game scored against a pitcher.

plate discipline – a hitter's ability to make good decisions at the plate by only swinging at pitches they can hit well.

record – a top achievement by a player.

rookie – a professional athlete in his or her first season in a sport.

ONLINE RESOURCES

To learn more about the Seattle Mariners, please visit **abdobooklinks.com** or scan this QR code. These links are routinely monitored and updated to provide the most current information available.

INDEX